SPACE
INFOGRAPHICS

By Harriet Brundle
Designed by Matt Rumbelow

BookLife
PUBLISHING

©BookLife Publishing 2019

Distributed by:
Independent Publishers Group
814 N. Franklin Street
Chicago, IL 60610

ISBN: 978-1-78637-634-3

Written by:
Harriet Brundle

Edited by:
Charlie Ogden

Designed by:
Matt Rumbelow

SPACE
Infographics

Contents

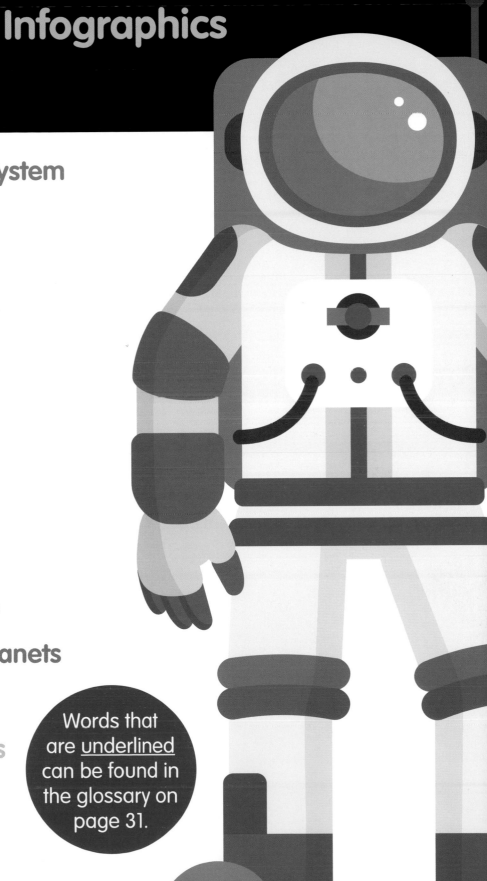

Words that are <u>underlined</u> can be found in the glossary on page 31.

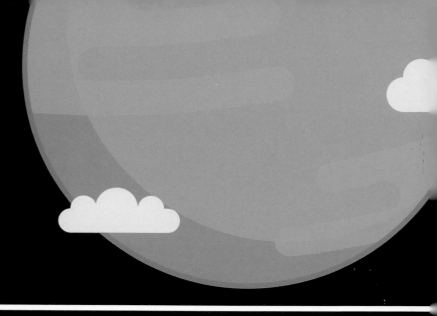

The Solar System

The Solar System is made up of the Sun as well as smaller parts that include planets, moons, <u>asteroids</u>, dwarf planets and <u>comets</u>.

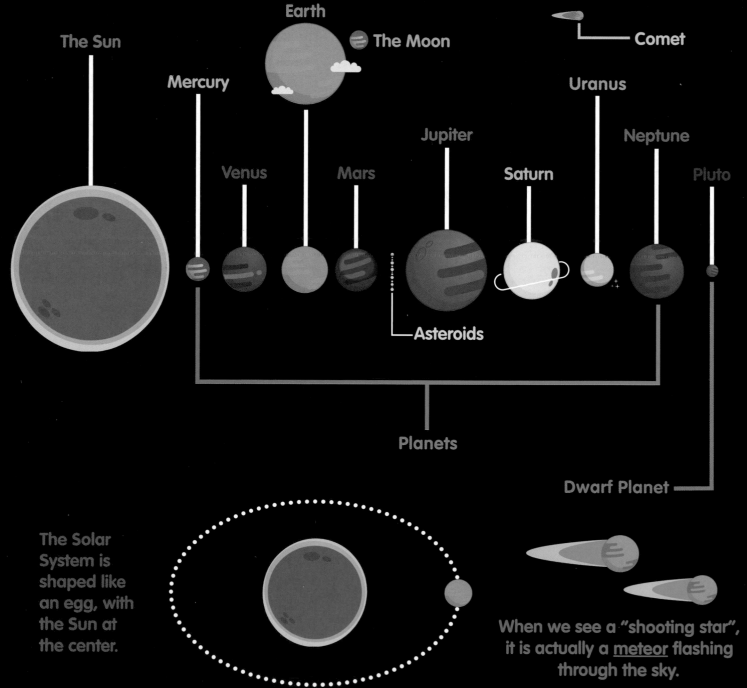

The Sun

Mercury

Earth

The Moon

Venus

Mars

Jupiter

Saturn

Comet

Uranus

Neptune

Pluto

Asteroids

Planets

Dwarf Planet

The Solar System is shaped like an egg, with the Sun at the center.

When we see a "shooting star", it is actually a <u>meteor</u> flashing through the sky.

4,600,000,000

Astronomers estimate that the Solar System is 4.6 billion years old. For many years, humans were unaware of the Solar System and thought that planet Earth was at the center of the universe.

The planets orbit around the Sun. Moons orbit around their planets.

Saturn

Titan

The Sun

53

Saturn has 53 named moons. The largest is called Titan.

The Sun contains 99.86% of the Solar System's mass. The remaining 0.14% is mostly made up by the planets.

Mass of the Sun

Mass of everything else

The Sun

The Sun is a star at the center of the Solar System. It is the largest object in the Solar System

The Sun is one of around 100 billion stars in our Galaxy.

The Sun

The Solar System

The Galaxy

100,000,000,000

The Sun is a ball of gas that gives off light and heat.

The Sun is the most important source of energy and light for life on Earth.

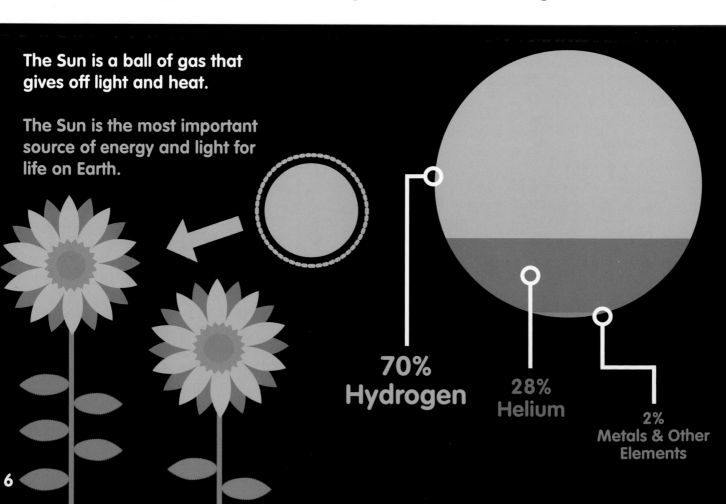

70% Hydrogen

28% Helium

2% Metals & Other Elements

The temperature at the center of the Sun is

27,000,000°F.

The Sun is 92.9 million miles (mi) away from Earth.

It takes around 8 minutes for light from the surface of the Sun to travel to Earth.

It would take 1.3 million planets the size of Earth to fill the volume of the Sun.

Mercury

Mercury is the planet closest to the Sun. It can be seen with the naked eye and is visible from Earth for much of the year.

❄ -279 ☀ 800

Mercury has the widest temperature extremes of all the planets, with possible temperatures ranging from -279°F to 800°F.

Mercury's surface is covered in <u>craters</u>. It has a thick, partly molten core and a thin outer crust. The surface looks very similar to the Earth's moon.

967 miles 220.6 yards

Mercury's biggest crater, the Caloris Basin, is bigger than Texas!

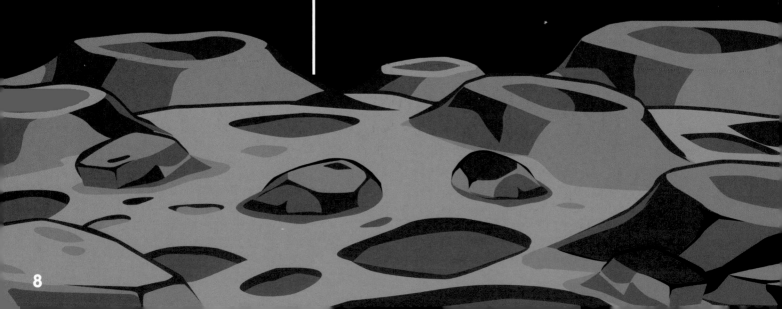

3,032

Mercury is the smallest planet in the Solar System. It has a diameter of 3,032 mi, making it around a third of the size of Earth.

10-15

Once every ten to fifteen years, Mercury can be seen crossing in front of the Sun. This event is known as a transit.

Mercury orbits the Sun once every 88 Earth days. It travels faster than any other planet at 31 mi per second.

Mercury has no atmosphere, which means that there is no weather on the planet at all.

Only two spacecraft have ever visited Mercury. It is very difficult to reach Mercury because it is so close to the Sun.

Venus

Venus is the second planet from the Sun. It is the brightest of all the planets and can be seen from Earth with the naked eye.

869°F

Venus has an extremely <u>dense</u> atmosphere that traps heat from the Sun. Temperatures on Venus can reach as high as **869°F**, making it the hottest planet in the Solar System.

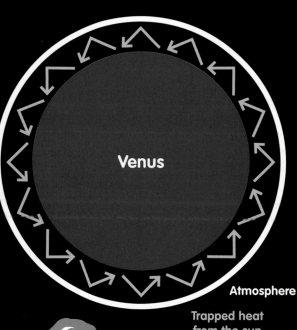

Venus

Atmosphere

Trapped heat from the sun

The surface of the planet is extremely dry and is covered in craters, mountains and volcanoes, some of which may be active today.

The planet Venus is named after the Roman goddess of love and beauty.

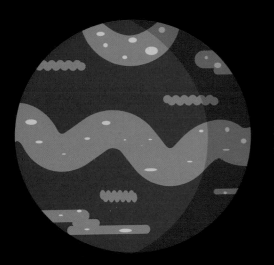
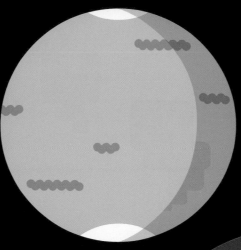

Venus and Earth are very similar in terms of size and mass.

The temperature on Venus is so hot that probes sent by scientists can only last 2 or 3 hours before they are destroyed by the heat.

7,521 mi

diameter of Venus

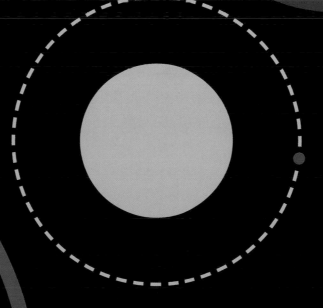

It takes Venus 225 Earth days to orbit around the Sun.

Venus is 67 million mi from the Sun.

Earth

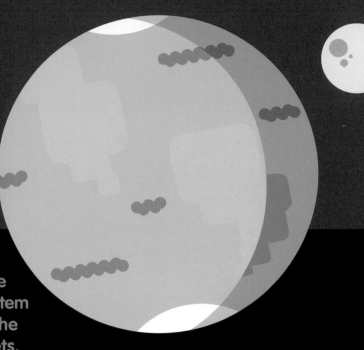

Earth is the third planet from the Sun and is believed to be the only planet in the Solar System that can support life. Earth is the largest of the <u>terrestrial planets</u>.

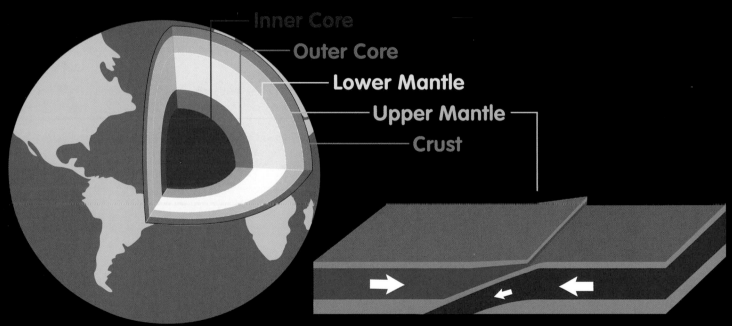

- Inner Core
- Outer Core
- **Lower Mantle**
- **Upper Mantle**
- Crust

The Earth's crust is split into parts, called tectonic plates, that float on the mantle. Tectonic plates move between 1 to 2 inches per year.

365

The Earth takes 365 days to orbit the Sun

93m

Earth is 93 million mi from the Sun.

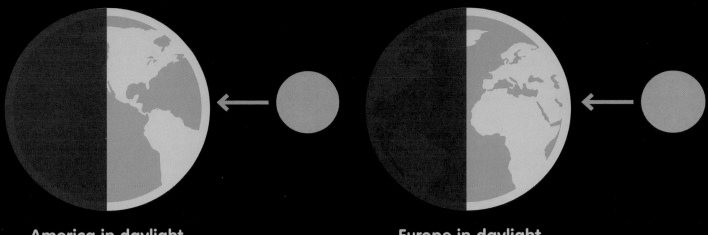

The Earth is constantly spinning on its <u>axis</u> and does one full rotation around every 24 hours. This is why we have night and day.

America in daylight

Europe in daylight

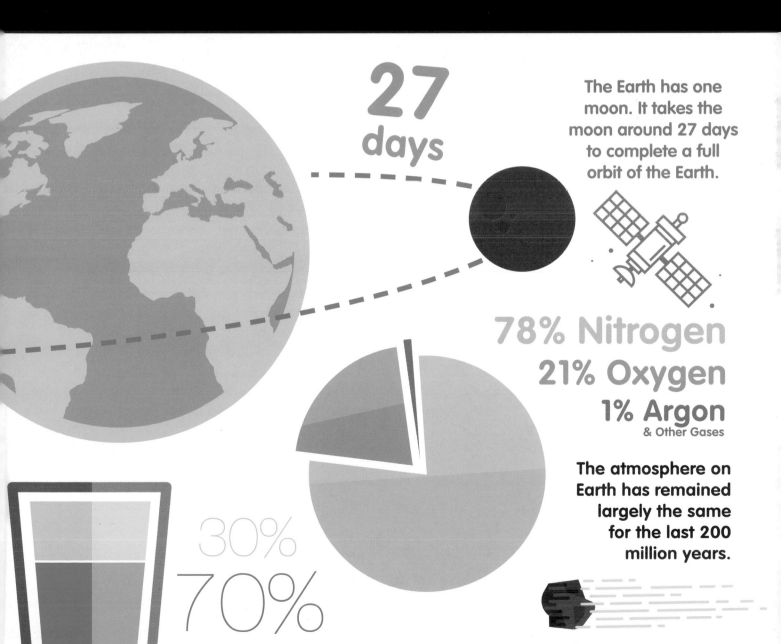

27 days

The Earth has one moon. It takes the moon around 27 days to complete a full orbit of the Earth.

78% Nitrogen
21% Oxygen
1% Argon
& Other Gases

The atmosphere on Earth has remained largely the same for the last 200 million years.

30%
70%

70% of the Earth's surface is covered by water.

4,500,000,000
Earth was formed around 4.5 billion years ago.

13

Mars

Mars is the fourth planet from the Sun. It is often referred to as 'the red planet' because of its red appearance.

128 - 154
million miles from the Sun.

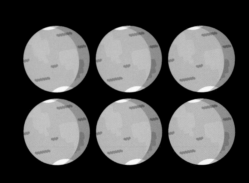

The diameter of Mars is 4,212 mi. It is approximately 6 times smaller than Earth.

Mars has clouds and wind, just like Earth. At times, the wind can blow the dust on the surface into a storm so big that it covers the entire planet!

The surface of Mars is dry and dusty. There are craters, canyons, volcanoes and mountains covering it.

Mars is the second most <u>hospitable</u> planet after Earth. Space missions are being planned and undertaken to increase our understanding of Mars.

The average temperature on Mars is -67°F.

Mars is named after the Roman god of war.

16.77 Mi

Mars is home to the biggest volcano in the Solar System, named Olympus Mons. It is 16.77 miles high and three times the size of Mount Everest.

Mt. Everest   Olympus Mons

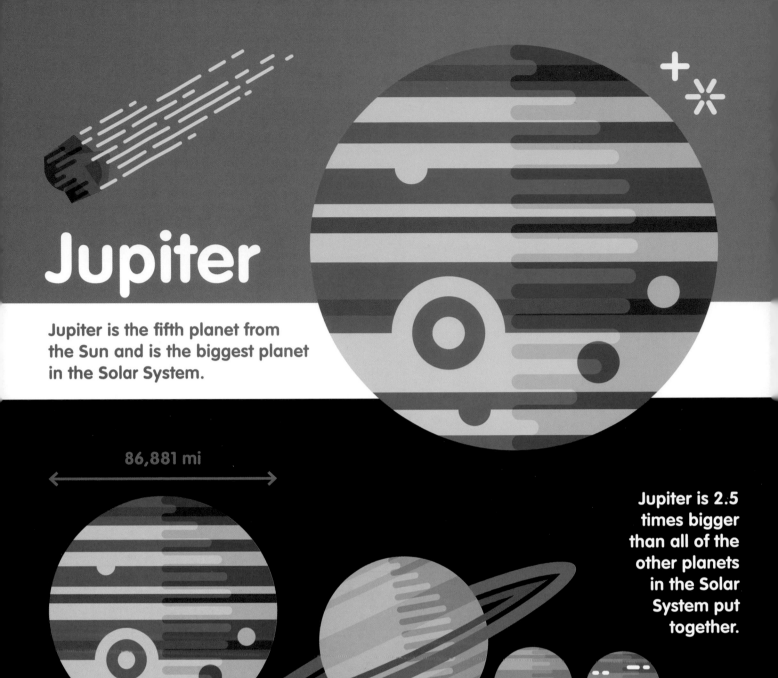

Jupiter

Jupiter is the fifth planet from the Sun and is the biggest planet in the Solar System.

86,881 mi

Jupiter is 2.5 times bigger than all of the other planets in the Solar System put together.

Jupiter is a gas planet. Its atmosphere is made mostly out of hydrogen and helium gas and the surface is covered in thick clouds.

Jupiter has narrow rings that are made out of dust and small pieces of rock.

The Great Red Spot is a storm similar to a <u>hurricane</u> that appeared on Jupiter around 400 years ago. The storm is large enough to be viewed from Earth with a telescope.

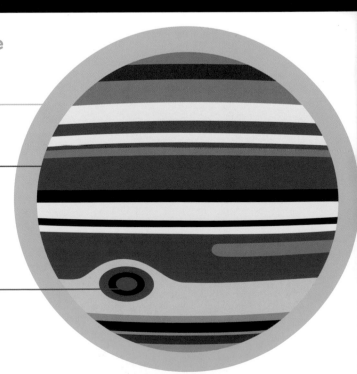

Jupiter spins faster than any other planet.
It completes a full rotation in just under 10 hours.

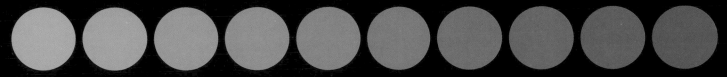

It takes Jupiter around 4,330 Earth days to orbit the Sun.

365 Days

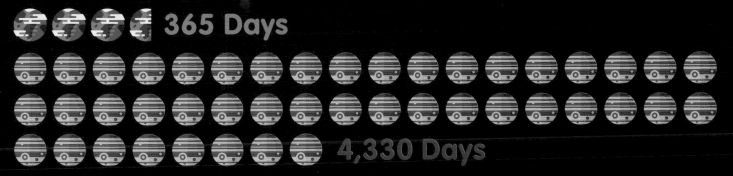

4,330 Days

Jupiter has over 60 known moons. Jupiter's largest moon is also the largest moon in the entire Solar System – it is named Ganymede.

More than 1000 Earths would fit inside Jupiter.

Saturn

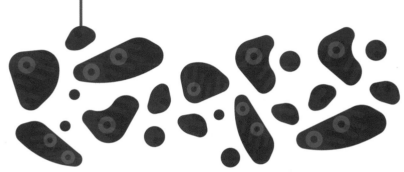

Saturn is the sixth planet from the Sun and is the second largest planet in the Solar System. It is the furthest planet from Earth that can be seen with the naked eye.

Galileo

Saturn is known for its impressive rings, which are mostly made out of billions of pieces of ice, dust and rocks. The rings were first discovered by Galileo Galilei over 400 years ago and stretch more than 7,891 mi from the planet.

Like Jupiter, Saturn is also a gas planet that is made almost entirely out of hydrogen and helium.

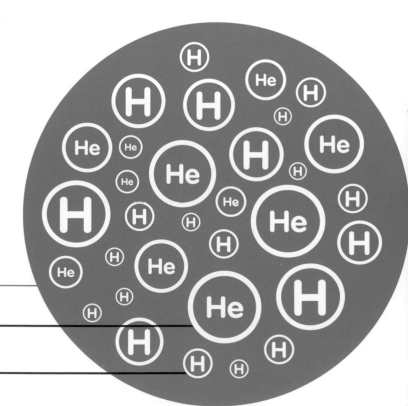

Helium

Hydrogen

Earth's orbit of the Sun

Saturn's orbit of the Sun

Saturn travels at an average speed of 21,637 miles per hour. That's around 15 times faster than a jumbo jet.

Saturn has over 60 moons, the largest of which is named Titan.

Saturn is spinning on an axis, just like Earth, meaning that it too experiences seasons. However, due to its distance from the Sun, the seasons are much more subtle than Earth's.

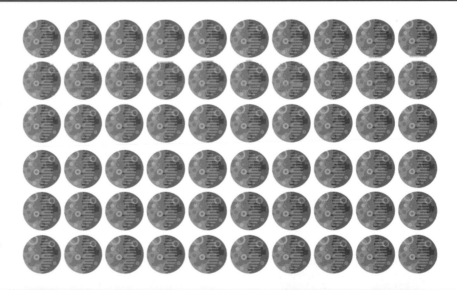

Saturn is 887.9 million mi from the Sun.

80 mins

8 mins

Saturn is so far from the Sun that it takes sunlight around an hour and twenty minutes to reach the planet.

Uranus

Uranus is the seventh planet from the Sun. It cannot be seen with the naked eye and was discovered in 1781 with a telescope.

98 degrees

Uranus is on an axis of 98 degrees, so it is almost horizontal as it orbits the sun. It takes 17 hours and 14 minutes for Uranus to complete a full rotation on its axis.

900

The wind speed on Uranus can reach 559 miles per hour (mph).

27

Uranus has 27 moons, which have mostly been named after a selection of Shakespearean characters.

Uranus has 11 inner rings and 2 outer rings, most of which are extremely narrow and dark in color. The rings are made out of a combination of small dust particles and large boulders.

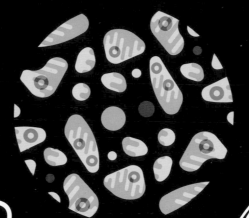

A spacecraft named Voyager 2 is the only spacecraft to have flown past Uranus; it was able to send back to Earth the first ever close-up images of the planet.

It takes Uranus 84 Earth years to orbit the Sun.

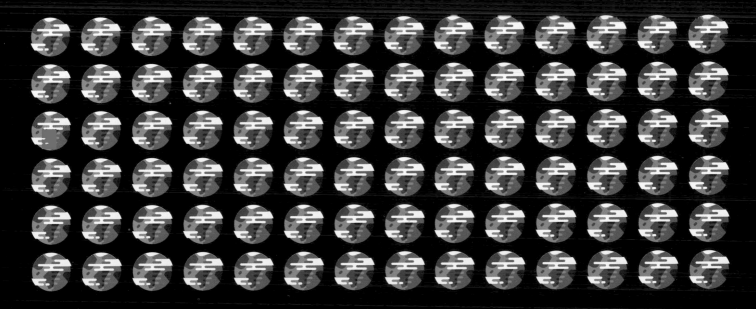

The average temperature in the cloud tops of Uranus is -356.8°F, making it one of the coldest planets in the Solar System.

Uranus -356.8°F

Earth 59°F

Neptune

Neptune is the eighth and furthest planet from the Sun. It cannot be seen without a telescope.

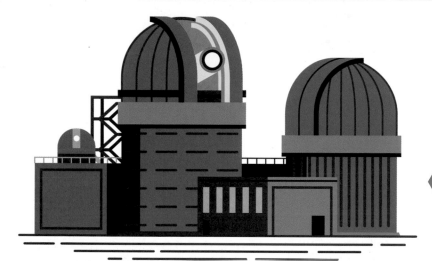

Neptune is the last of the gas planets and, like the others, it mostly consists of hydrogen, helium and methane. As with Uranus, it is this combination that gives Neptune its blue color.

 H Hydrogen **He** Helium **CH$_4$** Methane

The temperature on Neptune can fall as low as

-360°F

making it the coldest planet in the Solar System.

30,598 mi
The diameter of Neptune

Neptune takes 15 hours and 57 minutes to fully rotate on its axis.

1,491 mph

Similar to the Great Red Spot on Jupiter, Neptune had a Great Dark Spot. The storm was the size of Earth and had wind speeds of 1,491 mph, which are the fastest wind speeds ever recorded on a planet in the Solar System. The storm lasted for around 5 years.

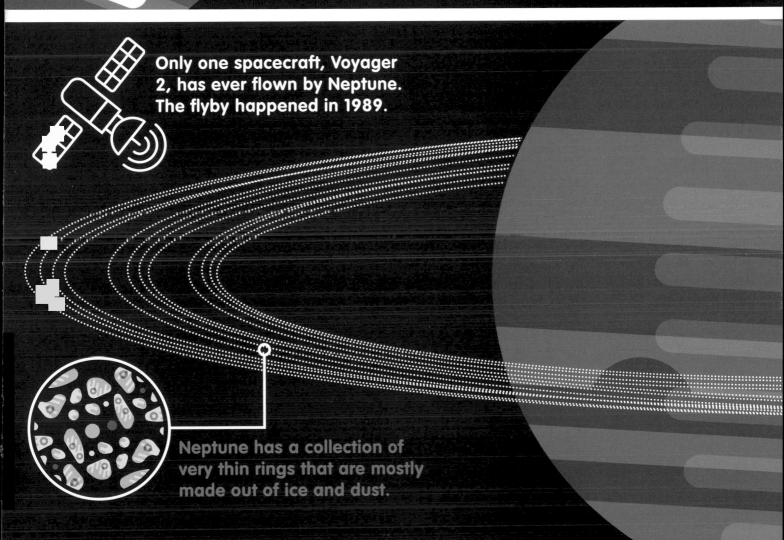

Only one spacecraft, Voyager 2, has ever flown by Neptune. The flyby happened in 1989.

Neptune has a collection of very thin rings that are mostly made out of ice and dust.

Neptune has 14 moons, one of which, named Triton, is as big as the dwarf planet Pluto.

Triton   **Pluto**

Pluto   Earth

Dwarf Planets

Dwarf planets are similar to planets, but are often much smaller. In order to be classified as a dwarf planet, the body must orbit around a star, assume an almost round shape and have other objects in its orbit, such as comets and asteroids.

The five main dwarf planets in the Solar System are named Ceres, Pluto, Eris, Haumea and Makemake.

Ceres
Located in the asteroid belt between Jupiter and Mars, this is the closest dwarf planet to Earth. It was also the first to be visited by a spacecraft. It measures 590 mi in diameter.

Pluto
Until recently, Pluto was classified as the ninth planet in the Solar System. The largest of the dwarf planets, Pluto is 1,474 mi in diameter and has an average surface temperature of -380°F.

Eris
First discovered in 2005, Eris was originally going to become the tenth planet, until both it and Pluto were named as dwarf planets. It takes Eris 557 Earth years to orbit around the Sun.

Haumea
A similar size to Pluto in length, Haumea is one of the fastest rotating large objects in the Solar System. Taking just 4 hours to complete a rotation, its extremely fast spinning is thought to be the reason why the planet has an unusual, elongated shape.

Makemake
Slightly smaller than Haumea, this dwarf planet was discovered in 2005. It takes 310 Earth years for Makemake to orbit the Sun. Makemake completes a rotation around its axis every 22.5 hours.

Pronounced "mah-kay-mah-kay"

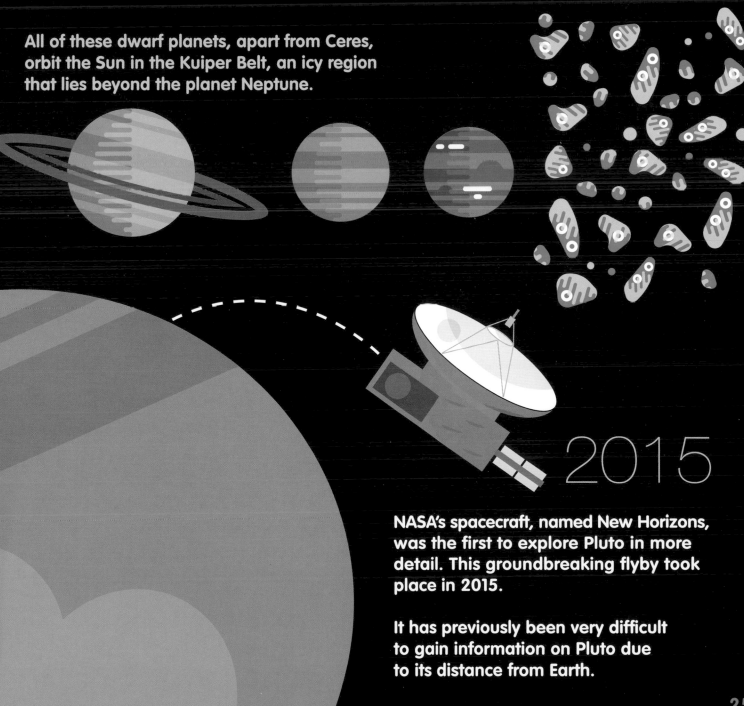

All of these dwarf planets, apart from Ceres, orbit the Sun in the Kuiper Belt, an icy region that lies beyond the planet Neptune.

2015

NASA's spacecraft, named New Horizons, was the first to explore Pluto in more detail. This groundbreaking flyby took place in 2015.

It has previously been very difficult to gain information on Pluto due to its distance from Earth.

Moons

There are more than 180 different moons in the Solar System. 173 moons orbit the planets in the Solar System.

Earth – 1 moon

The Earth's moon is the fifth largest in the Solar System. It is a large ball of rock that completes an orbit of the Earth every 27 days. Earth's moon is around 4.5 billion years old.

In 1969, Neil Armstrong was the first man to walk on the Earth's moon. He and his fellow astronaut, named Edwin Aldrin, walked around the Moon for several hours, collecting moon rocks and other samples.

Phobos

Deimos

Mars – 2 moons

Mars has two moons named Phobos and Deimos, which are among the smallest moons in the entire Solar System. They are covered in craters and dust.

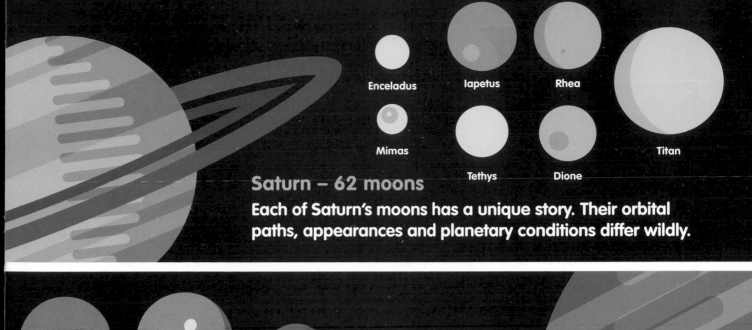

Enceladus Iapetus Rhea

Mimas Titan

Tethys Dione

Saturn – 62 moons

Each of Saturn's moons has a unique story. Their orbital paths, appearances and planetary conditions differ wildly.

Oberon Titania Umbriel Ariel Miranda

Uranus – 27 moons

Oberon and Titania are the largest of Uranus' moons and were both discovered in 1787. Many of Uranus' moons are very small and many still have little known about them.

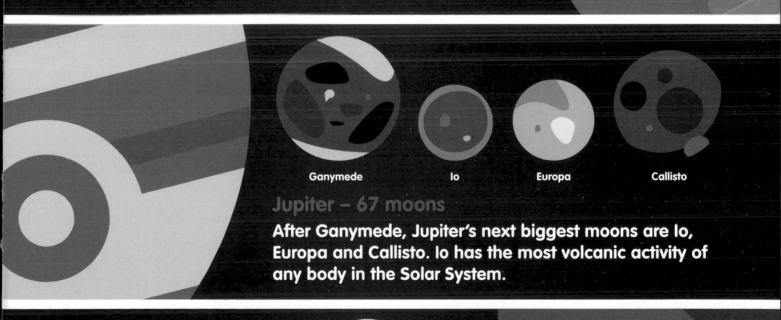

Ganymede Io Europa Callisto

Jupiter – 67 moons

After Ganymede, Jupiter's next biggest moons are Io, Europa and Callisto. Io has the most volcanic activity of any body in the Solar System.

Nereid Triton

Neptune – 14 moons

Triton, the largest of Neptune's moons, was the first to be discovered. It has an icy surface and is one of the coldest objects in the Solar System. The second largest of Neptune's moons, Nereid, was not discovered until one hundred years later. It is thought there are even more moons orbiting Neptune that have not been discovered yet.

Asteroids

Asteroids are rocky and irregularly shaped bodies that orbit around the Sun. They are too small to be called planets and are thought to be leftovers from the formation of the Solar System.

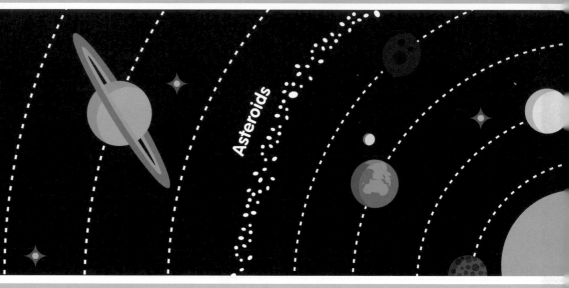

Asteroids

There are currently over 600,000 known asteroids in the Solar System.

× 1,000

Over 150 different asteroids are understood to have small moons that orbit them.

There are three main types of asteroid:

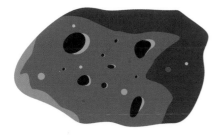

C type – made of clay and silicate rocks

S type – made of silicate material and <u>nickel-iron</u>

M type – made of nickel-iron

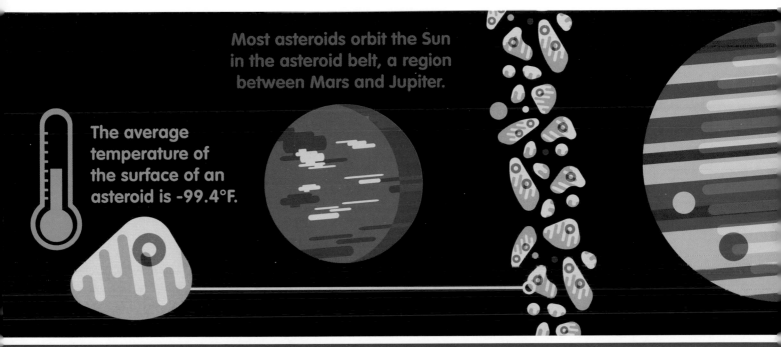

Most asteroids orbit the Sun in the asteroid belt, a region between Mars and Jupiter.

The average temperature of the surface of an asteroid is -99.4°F.

Since Earth formed over 4.5 billion years ago, asteroids have regularly come into contact with the surface of the planet. Smaller asteroids are believed to strike the Earth every 1,000 to 10,000 years.

It is thought that an asteroid impacting on Earth was partly to blame for the extinction of dinosaurs!

Space Quiz

1. How many of the planets can you name?
2. What are dwarf planets?
3. How many moons does Earth have?
4. What are asteroids?
5. Which planet is closest to the Sun?

True or False?

1. It takes Earth 365 days to orbit the Sun.
2. Mars is blue in color.
3. The planet Saturn has rings around it.
4. The Sun is a star.
5. The temperature on Venus is extremely cold.

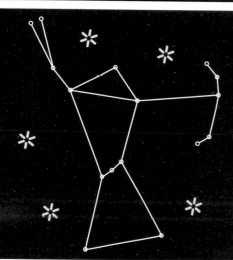

Find Orion's Belt!

Orion the hunter is one of the most recognizable <u>constellations</u>. At night time, go outside and look for three bright stars that are almost in a straight line. These three stars are Orion's belt. The two stars to the north of the belt are his shoulders and the two to the south are his feet!

Make your own planet!

1. Blow up a balloon.

2. Papier mâché the outside of the balloon with craft glue and strips of old newspaper.

3. When it has dried, pop the balloon and you are left with the base for your planet.

4. Paint and decorate your base to look like any planet you want.

Glossary

asteroids rocky and irregularly shaped bodies that orbit around the Sun

astronomers people who study the universe and the objects in space

axis the internal line around which an object spins, such as a planet or moon

comets small objects made out of ice and dust that, when near the heat of the sun, melt slightly to create long tails behind them

constellations groups of stars that form a recognizable pattern or image in the sky

craters holes in a planet or moon that are usually caused by a meteorite impact

dense lots of matter that has been very tightly squeezed together

galaxy many solar systems, stars and planets that all orbit around a central point, most commonly a black hole

hospitable good conditions for living or growing

hurricane a violent wind that has a circular movement

mass the amount of matter that a body or object contains

meteors pieces of rock or other matter that produce a bright light as they heat up in the atmosphere

nickel-iron a mix of metals that make up the majority of most planets' cores

orbit the path that a smaller object in space makes around a larger object in space, which is caused by gravity

terrestrial planets planets that have a rocky surface, such as Mercury, Venus, Earth and Mars

Index